Royal
SECRETS
&
SCANDALS

IMPORTANT DATES

800–1000s Early kingdoms of England, Scotland and Wales

1016–1066 English and Viking rulers in England

1066 Norman Conquest; William I ousts Harold II

1284 Wales ruled jointly with England

1377–1471 Later Plantagenets and Lancastrians including Richard II, Henry IV, Henry V and Henry VI

1450s–1485 Wars of the Roses in England between Lancastrians and Yorkists

1485–1603 Tudors: Henry VII, Henry VIII, Edward VI, Mary I, Elizabeth I

1642–1660 Civil war and Commonwealth in England (Cromwell)

1714–1837 Hanoverian: Georges I, II, III, IV and William IV

1910 onwards Windsors: George V, Edward VIII, George VI, Elizabeth II

843–1057 Early Scottish kings, including Macbeth and Duncan

1058 Malcolm III founds Canmore line in Scotland

1154–1377 Early Plantagenets including Henry II, John, Edward II, Edward III

1306–1437 Scotland's Houses of Bruce and Stewart

1437–1603 Later Stewarts (Stuarts) in Scotland including James II, Mary, James VI

1461–1485 Yorkist kings Edward IV, Edward V, Richard III

1603–1688 Stuarts in England and Scotland: James I, Charles I, Charles II, James II

1689–1714 House of Stuart and Orange: William III and Mary II, Anne

1837–1910 Saxe-Coburg-Gotha: Victoria, Edward VII

➤➤ The court of Elizabeth I, here shown watching the magician John Dee (whose advice she treasured despite strict laws against witchcraft and the use of the occult).

INTRODUCTION

From the earliest dynasties 1,500 years ago, Britain's royal story has been filled with rivalries, intrigues, secrets and scandals. Palace plots could be both personal and political, and the royal court was often a place of rumour and suspicion. A monarch's ruling passions might be violent, often unpredictable, and to cross the monarch usually meant disgrace or death. Royal secrets were closely guarded; those who betrayed them did so at their peril. Secret marriages, marital discord, illicit liaisons, family feuds and sibling squabbles, political deals, jealousy, ambition, revenge, demotions, disappointment, disappearances, assassinations, ruthless murders: all may be found within the pages of this book.

SAXONS AND NORMANS

The early royal history of the British kingdoms is awash with blood and intrigue. Treachery, murder and family feuds ran rampant through England, Scotland and Wales. Ruthless queens plotted for their sons. Brother fought brother, sons disputed with fathers.

A CORONATION SCANDAL

King Eadwig (Edwy), just 16, went missing from his coronation feast in 955. The archbishop who had crowned him, Dunstan, found him dallying with two women – a mother and daughter. Dunstan dragged the furious king away from his partners – an act for which he was never forgiven. Eadwig later married the daughter, Aelgifu.

THE WICKED STEPMOTHER

In 959, King Eadwig died. He was succeeded by his brother Edgar the Peaceable, whose reign ended in 975. Edgar left two princes: Edward (16) was the son of his first queen, and the younger, Ethelred (13), was the son of Edgar's widow Aelfthrytha. A dark deed followed: 'In this year King Edward was killed at the gap of Corfe on 18 March in the evening ... and no worse deed than this for the English people was committed since they first came to Britain.' So the *Anglo-Saxon Chronicle* described Edward's murder in 975. Aelfthrytha, with her son Ethelred, had been waiting at Corfe Castle in

▲ Saxon England, from *Orbis Terrae Compendiosa Descriptio*, published in 1587, a time when secrets and scandals concerned the powerful.

Dorset for her stepson Edward, who rode in alone. While bending to take the welcome cup, Edward was stabbed. His horse stampeded, dragging the wounded king to his death.

BRIBERY, MASSACRE AND BETRAYAL

Ethelred was named 'Unready' (*unraed* meaning 'evil counsel'). He scandalised the realm by first buying off Viking attackers and then ordering the St Brice's Day massacre, an attack of peaceful Danish settlers. Deaths included Gunnhild, sister of King Sweyn of Denmark. Sanctuary-seekers were burned alive inside an Oxford church.

ESCAPE TO HUNGARY

Ethelred's son Edmund Ironside took on the Vikings but was betrayed by Eadric Streona, a serial traitor to both the English and Danes. When the Danish Cnut became king on Edmund's death in 1016, Eadric advised him to kill the baby boys Ironside had left behind: Edward and Edmund Ætheling. Instead, they were spirited away secretly to Hungary. Eadric's double-dealing ended in 1017, when Cnut had him killed. His corpse was hurled over London Wall to rot.

RUTHLESS RELATIONS

Cnut died in 1035. Of his 'English' sons, Sweyn held Norway, and Harold had power in England. However, their stepmother Queen Emma plotted to gain the crown for her own son, Harthacnut. Earl Godwin of Wessex also plotted for himself. More of Emma's sons appeared from Normandy: Edward and Alfred, children of Ethelred. Godwin seized them. Alfred Ætheling was taken to Ely, where he was blinded and soon died. Edward, however, escaped back across the Channel.

◄◄ Corfe Castle, where in 975 Prince Edward was murdered.

CNUT'S WIVES

Though a shrewd ruler, Cnut unfortunately caused a dynastic problem by keeping two wives. His English wife, Aelgifu of Northampton, was married without Church sanction. Her children, Sweyn and Harold, were therefore considered illegitimate: rumour even had it that they were changelings, the sons of a priest and a shoemaker respectively. Cnut then also married, officially, Emma (also known as Aelgifu-Emma), widow of the former king Ethelred.

Harold ('Harefoot') ruled for four years before his half-brother Harthacnut gained the throne. When his grasping tax-collectors were lynched in Worcester, the king had the city burned down. He also had Harefoot's body dug up and flung into a bog. Dying drunk at a wedding in 1042, Harthacnut was unmourned.

A GLUT OF GODWINS

Earl Godwin now backed Edward (the 'Confessor'), who returned from Normandy and was given Godwin's daughter Edith for a wife. But the union proved childless, so rumours abounded: Edward had taken a vow of chastity; a hunting mishap had left him impotent; he was homosexual.

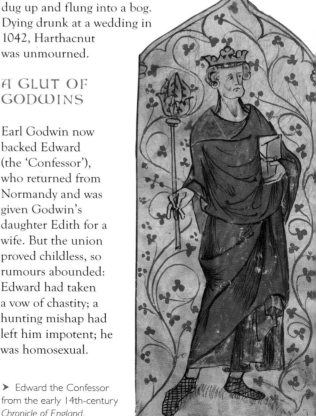

➤ Edward the Confessor from the early 14th-century *Chronicle of England*.

Godwin himself had lusty sons: Sweyn, Harold, Tostig, Gyrth, Leofwine and Wulfnoth. Surely one could make it to the throne? Sweyn's chance was lost when he shamefully abducted an abbess, and then murdered a cousin. He died in exile. Harold showed promise but, in 1051, the over-reaching Godwins were exiled. Soon back, they did their best to dislodge Edward's Norman henchmen. Then in 1053 Earl Godwin died, supposedly choking on bread after lying about his involvement in the murder of Alfred Ætheling. Divine judgement, whispered his enemies.

TRUTh UNDISCOVERED

In 1057 Edward Ætheling, the exiled son of King Edmund Ironside, returned from Hungary, but he died shortly afterwards – at which his followers cried foul. So in 1066, when Edward the Confessor also died, secrecy and suspicion surrounded the choice of Harold Godwinson (Earl Godwin's son) as king. What was the truth? Had the dying Confessor promised Harold the crown? Had Harold forced such a promise? Or was Duke William of Normandy right to claim Harold had sworn not to oppose William's bid for England?

William's victory at Hastings decided the issue, and the Normans claimed God's retribution on Harold the oath-breaker. Oath-breaking could be disastrous: William's son Henry I once pushed a man from the top of Rouen Castle for breaking his oath of allegiance.

Henry I sought safety in numbers. His string of mistresses produced more illegitimate children for him (at least 20) than any other English king. But his only son and heir drowned in 1120, so – after an untidy and brutal civil war – Henry II came to the throne, first of the Plantagenets.

▼ Detail from the Bayeux Tapestry showing Harold II crowned 'King of the English' at Westminster Abbey in 1066.

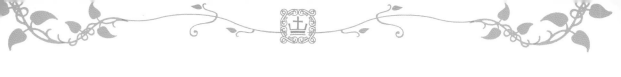

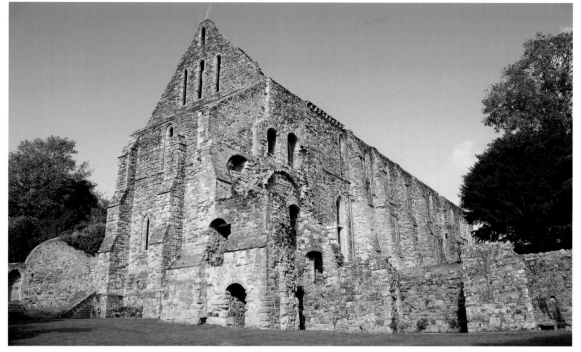

⌃ The ruins of Battle Abbey, near the site of the Battle of Hastings, where Harold was buried.

DUBIOUS DEATH

William I's private life was blameless – unlike that of his son, William Rufus. Unruly, possibly homosexual, 'loose-living', long-haired – such were the charges levelled at the king by a scandalised Church. A stray arrow during a New Forest hunt killed William Rufus in 1100. Walter Tyrrel took the blame, but William's brother Henry – also hunting that day – took the advantage and seized the throne. Older brother (and rival) Robert was kept as Henry's life-long prisoner.

➤ A Victorian interpretation of the death of William Rufus.

THE PLANTAGENETS

The royal marriage-go-round accelerated through the Plantagenet years in England and the early Stuart years in Scotland, where Robert II (1371–1390) could match England's Henry I for offspring. But of Robert's 21 children, 13 were legitimate. Royal marriages were arranged and publicly sanctioned by the Church. Secret marriages were barred, but not extra-marital affairs.

LOVERS AND SONS

Henry II married Europe's greatest heiress, the redoubtable Eleanor of Aquitaine, ex-wife of the King of France, in 1152. Together they had eight children, but Henry's publicly declared love for Rosamund Clifford around 1174 soured their marriage. Eleanor took revenge on Henry by siding with her sons against him.

WEB OF MYSTERY

Henry II hid 'Fair Rosamund' at Woodstock in a 'secret chamber', described in song and legend as 'a maze'. Her death in around 1176 gave rise to many tales: a jealous Queen Eleanor had bled Rosamund to death in a bath; she had been assassinated with a dagger or poison; the queen found a path through the maze to her prey by means of a silken thread. The love triangle featured in many troubadour songs and poems of the time.

AWAY WITH THEM ALL

Henry's son Richard I was a soldier of romance, but his wars cost a fortune, and he left his wife Berengaria childless, amid whispers of homosexual love for his father's enemy, Philip of France. Meanwhile, brother John plotted. In 1203 the king's nephew Arthur of Brittany, favoured to succeed Richard, 'disappeared'. Many believed that

INFAMY AND SHAME

Henry II's very public row with his Archbishop, Thomas Becket, caused a Europe-wide scandal when, in 1170, the churchman was slain in his cathedral by four knights acting on what they took to be Henry's command. The king did penance and Becket became a saint, his tomb a shrine for pilgrims.

▼ The murder of Thomas Becket (1170) shown in a psalter of 1220.

John had murdered him and had the body tossed into the River Seine. Trusted by nobody (even after Magna Carta, sealed in 1215), John created a final scandal in 1216 by losing his own Crown Jewels in the quicksands of the Wash.

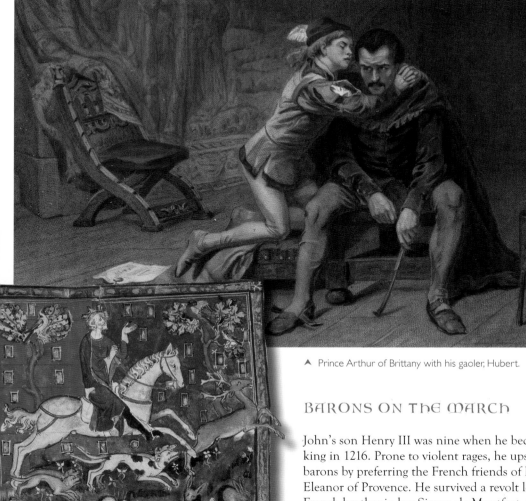

▲ Prince Arthur of Brittany with his gaoler, Hubert.

▲ King John, hunting, from a 14th-century miniature.

MATILDA DE BRIOUSE

Matilda was the wife of William de Briouse (or Braose), a friend of King John. Speaking indiscreetly about Arthur of Brittany's death, she aroused John's wrath. William fled, leaving Matilda and her son to be imprisoned in Windsor Castle where, in 1210, they were starved to death by royal command.

BARONS ON THE MARCH

John's son Henry III was nine when he became king in 1216. Prone to violent rages, he upset his barons by preferring the French friends of his wife Eleanor of Provence. He survived a revolt led by his French brother-in-law Simon de Montfort, 6th Earl of Leicester, thanks largely to young Prince Edward, the future Edward I.

UNKINGLY KING

Edward the soldier may have hammered rebels and Scots, but his son Edward II was of different mettle. Entranced by the handsome Piers Gaveston, a nobleman of Gascon origin, Edward further scandalised the barons by his eccentric 'low' pursuits (such as farming, digging, thatching – and rowing). At his coronation the king shared a couch with Gaveston, not the queen, while the couple's wedding presents also found their way to the royal favourite. In 1312 came the barons' revenge. They arrested Gaveston, who was duly butchered.

The She-Wolf's Revenge

Defeat by the Scots at Bannockburn in 1314 was a further blow to Edward II, who promoted new favourites, the Despensers (father and son). As mutiny spread, Queen Isabella left for France. There she scandalised her brother the king by taking a lover, Roger Mortimer. The pair returned to England in 1326 with Isabella, the 'She-Wolf', bent on vengeance. King Edward II was disposed of – murdered horribly, it was believed, at Berkeley Castle. Yet in turn his young son, Edward III, speedily rid himself of Mortimer, by execution in 1330, and sent his mother into retirement.

▲ Robert the Bruce's defeat of Edward II's army in 1314 humiliated the English King.

ALICE'S AVARICE

In his dotage, Edward III was at the mercy of his mistress, Alice Perrers, who received lavish gifts. In 1376 the Commons' Speaker declared 'it would be a great profit to the kingdom to remove that lady from the king's company so that the king's treasure could be applied to the war'. Instead, when Edward died in 1377, greedy Alice is said to have stripped the rings from the dead man's fingers.

Confusion and Coup

Richard II was ten when he came to the throne in 1377. He survived the Peasants' Revolt of 1381, but was then accused of tyranny. He was ousted by his cousin, Bolingbroke, who became Henry IV. In 1400, Richard was either murdered or starved to death at Pontefract.

Madness and Melancholy

Suspicious, secretive, and guilt-ridden after seizing the throne, Henry IV was also tormented by the waywardness of his son. Yet Prince Hal became King Henry V, victor at Agincourt in 1415. His French royal wife Catherine of Valois may have passed on her father's mental instability to their son, Henry VI. Henry – pious but with fits of melancholy madness – was a hapless pawn in the Wars of the Roses until put to death in the Tower of London by Yorkist enemies.

▼ Edward III with his son, Edward the Black Prince.

STRANGE CONFINEMENT

Henry VI's wife was Margaret of Anjou. When their son was born – after eight years of marriage and during one of Henry's bouts of melancholia – the king expressed bewilderment. The boy, he said, must have been conceived by the Holy Ghost. The prudish king once stormed out of 'a dance or show of young ladies with bared bosoms' during a Christmas entertainment.

A LADIES' MAN

The York victor, Edward IV, turned from battle to bed-hopping. In 1464 he secretly married Elizabeth Woodville, a widow (and the first English queen since 1066), after she refused to be his mistress. Her relatives profited shamelessly: John Woodville, aged about 20, was married to the Duchess of Norfolk – 'a slip of a girl about 80 years old'.

▼ A 19th-century depiction of the Princes in the Tower.

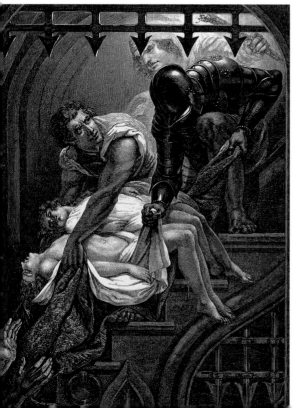

DEATHLY SECRETS

Edward IV liked food, drink and older ladies, growing fat in the arms of Jane Shore, 'the merriest of his concubines'. His brother Richard dealt with embarrassments – such as their unreliable brother Clarence, by tradition drowned in a wine butt at the Tower of London. In 1483 Edward IV died, whereupon Richard seized his two sons, enshrined in legend as the murdered Princes in the Tower. Their uncle, having had the boys declared illegitimate, became Richard III. After his death at Bosworth in 1485, Richard's remains were lost until 2012, when they were unearthed in a Leicester car park.

▲ The walls of the Tower of London enclosed many dark secrets.

JANE SHORE

On Edward IV's death, his mistress Jane Shore found a protector in Lord Hastings, until he was executed by Richard III. She was then accused of sorcery and did public penance as a harlot. The Marquis of Dorset, her next protector, was arrested for treason. Jane later married Thomas Lynom, but died poor and alone.

The TUDORS

▲ In this scene, Queen Catherine pleads before her unmoved husband King Henry VIII, who is desperate to be rid of her.

enry Tudor, victor at Bosworth, feared the throne he occupied as Henry VII would be claimed by others. His own claim derived from Owen Tudor, the grandfather who had secretly married Henry V's widow, Catherine; and through his mother, directly descended from Edward III. In 1486 Henry married his cousin, Elizabeth of York, daughter of Edward IV. She was eight years his senior, but their political union proved happy, until she died, in childbirth, in 1503, a year after their eldest son Prince Arthur's death.

WARWICK OR WARBECK?

Richard III had overlooked another nephew, Warwick, son of Clarence. Aged 10 at the time of the battle of Bosworth, Henry VII sent the boy to the Tower, but in 1486 came news of a youth claiming to be Warwick, escaped from prison. The well-rehearsed impostor was actually a boy named Lambert Simnel, though he was crowned 'Edward VI' in Ireland in 1487. After defeat in battle, he was employed as a turn-spit in the royal kitchens. The real Warwick was later executed, along with the more serious 'pretender', Perkin Warbeck, who declared himself 'Richard IV'.

▼ Young Henry VIII with his brother Arthur and sister Margaret.

SUPERKING

Henry VIII, king from 1509, scandalised Europe by throwing off the authority of the Pope, and disposing of four of his six wives. With kingship thrust on him by the death of his brother Arthur, Henry acted dutifully in marrying Arthur's widow, Catherine of Aragon. But when the desired son did not appear, Henry took drastic action. Initially shy with ladies, the king sought consolation at Court with a mistress or two. Bessie Blount bore him a son, Henry Fitzroy, but with still no legitimate heir, Henry pursued his 'great matter' – divorce from Catherine – against all opposition. Henry had already enjoyed an affair with Mary Boleyn when his eye fell on her sister Anne, who insisted Henry marry her.

SECRET PLEASURES

Henry VIII's courtship of Anne Boleyn was intense. He wrote her passionate letters, longing to be 'in my sweetheart's arms' (and also to kiss her breasts). When told of Catherine's death, he celebrated joyously, bedecked in yellow suiting, with a Mass and a banquet with dancing.

▲ Henry VIII woos Anne Boleyn, somewhat publicly.

Jane Seymour, Henry's third wife, perhaps had his real affection and produced the longed-for heir, Edward VI, at the cost of her life. Chosen on the strength of a portrait, Anne of Cleves was rejected on sight. The king refused to sleep with her. Flighty, naive Catherine Howard was half the age of Henry, who by then was bloated, sick and long past his sexual peak. With the young queen's secret flirtations soon exposed, she lost her head. Finally, the king found some peace with his twice-widowed sixth wife, Catherine Parr.

▼ Edward VI, the only legitimate son of Henry VIII.

LOST CROWNED HEADS

Anne Boleyn bewitched Henry – literally, or so her enemies said. She persuaded him to part from Catherine in 1531 and was pregnant by January 1533, when Henry secretly married her to ensure the child's legitimacy. After she too failed to bear a healthy son, passion turned to hatred. Accused of serial adultery and incest, Anne was beheaded for treason.

RELIGIOUS EXTREMES

Edward VI and his sister Mary I were religiously doctrinaire – he Protestant, she Catholic. The realm swirled with plots and counter-plots, while martyrs were made as men and women died for their faith. Mary married Catholic Philip of Spain, but no hoped-for child was born. The Venetian ambassador noted Mary's pallor and 'very deep melancholy', her constant weeping was attributed to 'menstruous retention'. She was bled regularly. Philip was an absentee spouse; two 'pregnancies' proved false and Mary died disappointed.

SURVIVING RUMOUR

Elizabeth, Anne Boleyn's disregarded daughter, was largely ignored by her father and targeted by ambitious 'protectors' including Thomas Seymour, who scandalised her attendants by frolics in the teenager's bedroom. As queen, from 1558, Elizabeth knew how to survive scandal, keeping her own counsel, and virginity, intact. Her suitors included Robert Dudley, Earl of Leicester, whose reputation was ruined after his wife Amy Robsart fell fatally downstairs – by accident or design? The scandal dashed any chance of his ever sharing the throne, though he retained Elizabeth's affection. All other suitors were kept dangling, including the foreign contingent, of whom François, Duke of Alençon, her 'little frog', was favourite.

FALL FROM GRACE

Amy Robsart married the Earl of Leicester at 18. He was Queen Elizabeth's favourite, named as Protector of the Realm, and it was said the two would marry – despite his wife's existence. In 1560, Dudley was at Court; Amy at Cumnor Place, rented by her husband's friend. On 8 September, it was said that she sent the entire household off to Abingdon Fair. They returned to find her dead at the foot of the stairs.

◄ Robert Dudley, Earl of Leicester.

MYSTERY IMAGES

Elizabethans loved codes, ciphers and invisible ink, extending the use of secret signs and images to poetry and art. The queen's image was defined by portraits. She took enormous care over her appearance, wigs and all, and loved silk stockings 'pleasant, fine and delicate' rather than common cloth, though she was less keen to take baths. The Rainbow portrait (held at Hatfield House), for example, is notably rich in imagery, covered with secret symbols (such as eyes and ears) and mythical allusions that transform the woman Elizabeth into the mythical queen Gloriana.

➤ The Rainbow Portrait of Elizabeth I (about 1602).

SPIES, CIPHERS AND SECRET MESSAGES

Elizabeth's safety was ensured by her spymaster, Sir Francis Walsingham. His agents uncovered numerous plots, including those of William Parry (1585) and Anthony Babington (1586), which put Mary, Queen of Scots' head on the block. Walsingham paid his spies, one of whom was probably the playwright Christopher Marlowe, largely out of his own pocket.

NO PUBLICITY

High-fliers at Court risked all by defying the queen. Walter Raleigh fell into disgrace for marrying Bess Throckmorton without the queen's permission. The pair had wed in secret; when the queen found out, they were sent to the Tower. Both survived, though Raleigh later fell foul of James I, and was beheaded in 1618.

LETTICE'S LOVES

Lettice Knollys (1543–1634) attracted scandal. Married at 17 to the Earl of Essex, Lettice was also close to Elizabeth I's favourite, Robert Dudley, Earl of Leicester. Gossips accused Dudley of poisoning Essex to marry Lettice, which he did in 1578. Nobody dared tell the queen for almost a year. When Leicester himself died, in 1588, it was said Lettice had poisoned him to wed his gentleman-of-the-horse, Christopher Blount. Lettice's son, Robert Devereux, became the ageing queen's favourite, before his failed rebellion in 1601; both he and his step-father Blount were executed. Lettice survived into the Stuart era, fighting in court to save her fortune from an illegitimate son of Dudley's.

◄ Sir Walter Raleigh, courtier, adventurer and favourite of Queen Elizabeth. He fell from grace when James I became king.

▼ Robert Devereux, 2nd Earl of Essex. Son of a scandal-tainted mother, he let ambition overrule reason, and lost his head in 1601.

THE STUARTS

Few royal dramas matched Mary Stuart's. The Queen of Scots was implicated in two murders – that of her secretary Rizzio (a crime orchestrated by her husband, Lord Darnley) and of Darnley himself, found dead at his blown-up Edinburgh house. Mary then ran away with – or was abducted by – the presumed murderer, the Earl of Bothwell. After her abdication came exile in England, where Elizabeth I's spies gathered evidence of plots by Mary against the English queen. The net closed in 1587, when Elizabeth signed Mary's death warrant. Execution followed.

▲ Mary, Queen of Scots, caught in a web of plots, was finally snared by the wiles of Elizabeth's spymaster Walsingham.

SECRET BURIALS

Mary's clothes were burnt (there were to be no 'relics' to venerate) and her blood-soaked dog washed after lying devotedly beside her corpse. First buried at Peterborough, Mary Stuart's body was moved in 1612 to Westminster Abbey where, in 1867, the tomb was opened. Inside lay pathetic Stuart baby-coffins, including those of the children of James II and Queen Anne. Also in the vault was Arbella Stuart, known to Mary in childhood.

THE DISMAL HISTORY OF ARBELLA STUART

Arbella Stuart posed a threat to Elizabeth I and James VI/I, being of both Stuart and Tudor descent. So she was kept under virtual house-arrest with her grandmother, Bess of Hardwick, and given unfulfilled promises of a 'good marriage'. Desperate, in 1602 Arbella offered to marry a man she had never met – Edward Seymour – but he too had a claim to the throne so the plan was scotched. Finally allowed at Court, in 1610, Arbella secretly married Seymour's brother, William. The pair were arrested, but escaped. However, Arbella (dressed as a man) was captured on the Thames and ended her days in the Tower.

➤ Arbella Stuart.

▼ Hardwick Hall, where Arbella was virtually held prisoner.

▲ Gunpowder plotters hauled to public execution in London.

SCANDAL AT COURT

James I (James VI of Scotland) had a Danish wife, and fathered sons, but his effusive weakness for young men, notably the Duke of Buckingham (whom he called 'Steenie'), raised eyebrows. So did the king's fear of witchcraft, dating from at least 1590, when 'witches' in North Berwick were accused of conspiring with the Devil to kill him. The Gunpowder Plot of 1605, to blow up Parliament, James claimed to have discovered himself. In fact, a mysterious informer revealed all.

CHARLES, FATHER AND SON

Charles I, an exemplary family man, was ill-suited to cope with a restless Parliament, but ruling without it led to civil war. The king's execution in 1649, horrifying Europe, sent his heir on the run. Charles II hid in an oak tree after the battle of Worcester in 1651, donning servants' clothes to be smuggled abroad. With soot-smudged face and cut-off curls, he struggled to disguise his height in shoes which were painfully small.

▲ Portrait of Charles II.

Narrow escapes made good stories after the Restoration in 1660, when the 'merry monarch' could enjoy himself. In 1662, the king travelled to Portsmouth to meet his bride, Catherine of Braganza, later admitting he was thankful for not being required to consummate the union that night as 'matters would have gone very sleepily'. Catherine spoke only Portuguese, and her ladies-in-waiting were considered plain. Charles soon remedied this by adding his mistresses to her entourage.

The Royal Mistresses

Barbara Villiers (1640–1709) started her amatory career at 16 with the Earl of Chesterfield, continuing the association when she later married Roger Palmer. In 1660 she arrived at Charles II's Court, exiled in Brussels, and became a royal mistress. At the Restoration, her husband, now Earl of Castlemaine, discreetly 'retired', leaving Barbara free to host parties, accept bribes from diplomats, and amuse the king.

Among Charles II's other mistresses were Lucy Walter, Louise de Kéroualle, Moll Davis and Nell Gwynn. Each had her own story, none more 'rags to riches' than Nell's: raised in a bawdyhouse, self-educated, and a comedy star at Drury Lane, she assiduously promoted her royal sons, the Duke of St Albans and Lord Beauclerc. Charles's mistresses were not thought particularly scandalous, though Kéroualle did raise eyebrows with her mock 'wedding' to the king in 1671, before providing him with another son, Charles Lennox, Duke of Richmond.

▲ James II.

James II

James II, lacking his brother's charm, nevertheless shared his sexual appetite. He had two wives, and four children with Arabella Churchill, sister of John, the future Duke of Marlborough. James's interest flared, said scandalmongers, when a fall from her horse exposed the lady's attractions.

▲ Nell Gywnn was a popular figure.

CASTLEMAINE'S SHAME

Widowed in 1705, Barbara Villiers, Lady Castlemaine, married a rake named Beau Fielding, who proved to have wedded another woman two weeks previously. The humiliating court case dimmed Castlemaine's lustre, and hastened her death.

WARMING-PAN BABY

James's first wife, the Protestant Anne Hyde, had two daughters (Mary and Anne). News of a son, born in 1688 to the king's new Catholic wife, Mary of Modena, caused uproar. A Catholic heir was unwelcome. Tales spread of the boy being smuggled into the queen's chamber in a warming pan. The birth of the 'Old Pretender' (James III to his Jacobite supporters) sparked the Glorious Revolution and ended James II's reign.

➤ Mary of Modena, the wife of James II, who allegedly smuggled her son and heir in a warming pan.

SECRETS AND SPIES

Princess Mary, at 15, burst into tears when told she was to marry her Dutch cousin, William of Orange. He was asthmatic, taciturn, and 'seldom cheerful'. But she did her duty and the marriage survived, although William's mistresses included her own friend, Elizabeth Villiers. In 1685, the Villiers affair was made public when spies in the royal Dutch household told Mary's father, King James. William discovered the situation from letters intercepted on their way to England and patched matters up. From 1688, William and Mary reigned jointly, James II having been exiled. Mary remained a loyal wife and her death from smallpox left William grief-stricken.

◄ Mary, wife of William III and daughter of James II.

BEST OF FRIENDS

Mary's sister Anne (queen from 1702) had a devoted friend, Sarah Jennings (secretly married to John Churchill in 1678), exchanging letters with her as 'Mrs Morley' (Anne) and 'Mrs Freeman' (Sarah). Sarah's influence grew, as war hero Churchill became Duke of Marlborough, until in 1707 she was supplanted in the queen's affections by Abigail Masham. Domestic, conservative and fond of tea, Queen Anne presided over intrigues by her politicians, who faced a succession problem. Anne had no surviving child, despite 18 pregnancies. Were the Catholic Stuarts to be recalled? The government decided otherwise, so at Anne's death the crown passed to the Protestant George of Hanover, the great-grandson of James I.

▲ Sarah, Duchess of Marlborough.

The Hanoverians

The Georgians arrived with a murky past. George I, Elector of Hanover, was shrewd, shy, suspicious, brave and said little. He brought to Britain two famously ugly mistresses, the skinny Ehrengard (nicknamed the Maypole) and fat Charlotte (the Elephant) – who may also have been his half-sister. George kept his wife, Sophia Dorothea, locked up. Bored with her husband, Sophia had turned to a Swedish count, who in 1694 'disappeared' for good. Whisperers claimed his body had been hacked up and buried under the floorboards of the Herrenhausen, George's country retreat. Sophia was divorced, never allowed to see her children again, and stayed locked up until her death, 32 years later.

People mocked George for failing to conform to the British idea of a king. He spent evenings with Ehrengard, cutting out paper patterns, and disliked clever women like his daughter-in-law, Caroline. Government was largely left to the wily Robert Walpole, who presided over the century's most sensational financial crash, the South Sea Bubble.

GENERATION GAP

The Hanoverians had a special father-son relationship – mutual hatred. George II could not forgive his father for depriving him of his mother at 11. He wanted his father dead, in order to free her, but Sophia died in 1726. George I celebrated her death by visiting the Haymarket Theatre, then waited seven months before going to Hanover to bury her. He died on the way.

GEORGE II

George II and his clever wife Caroline of Ansbach seemed to hate their son Frederick from the start. They also disliked his wife, Augusta of Saxe-Gotha, despite choosing her themselves. Yet Frederick was popular. 'Fretz's popularity makes me vomit,'

exploded the king. For years, father and son met only at christenings, when rows resulted. George once demanded his son's arrest. Frederick declared that George had 'an insatiable sexual appetite', which seems to have been true. Yet George II got on well with Caroline, his wife, a lively flirt (rumours abounded of an affair with Walpole), and was heartbroken when she died in 1737. The king died in 1760, of a heart attack in the lavatory.

▲ The last public beheading in England (1747). Lord Lovat betrayed the House of Hanover to support the Stuart claim to the throne and was convicted of treason.

FARMER GEORGE

George III was born in lodgings after his grandfather evicted his parents – Frederick and Augusta – from their palace apartments. George III fell in love with Sarah Lennox, descended from a mistress of Charles II, but gave her up for a German princess. A decent man, he restored the Court's reputation, surviving the loss of the American colonies and bouts of 'madness' caused by porphyria (with its ghastly medical 'treatments') to retain his people's affection.

➤ In a Charles Williams caricature (1803) 'Farmer George' (George III) confronts rival gardener 'Napoleon'.

◀ The South Sea Bubble (1720) was inflated by its promoters. Here, John Blunt, one of the investment scheme's frontmen, encourages would-be investors.

STORMS IN EXILE

The Hanoverians survived Stuart Jacobite attempts to remove them, in 1715 and 1745, and Charles Edward Stuart ('Bonnie Prince Charlie') lived in exile after Culloden (1746). His mistresses included his cousin Louise de Montbazon (deserted when pregnant), and Clementina Walkenshaw, whose daughter Charlotte he refused to legitimise. At 51, in 1772, he married a 19-year-old. When he refused his daughter Charlotte permission to marry lawfully, she took a lover, a French archbishop. Her three children were kept secret.

GEORGE IV

George IV acted as Prince Regent from 1812–20, during his father's illness. He was the opposite of George III. Tall and dignified in youth, he ate and drank his way to obesity. Cartoonists lampooned his scandalous behaviour and increasingly gross appearance, but society climbers found George to their taste. He was gifted, charming, and could rise to the occasion with great dignity when required. The fashionista Beau Brummel reflected that he could have been the best comic actor in Europe. George certainly enjoyed mimicking his father. He found it less amusing when Brummel made a joke about him – shouting 'who's your fat friend?' at the king's departing back – and he never spoke to Brummel again.

▲ A 1792 caricature by James Gillray, the 'Horrors of Digestion', portrays George IV as an obese and gluttonous Prince of Wales.

▲ George IV could strike a handsome pose.

SECRET MARRIAGE

George IV had affairs with Perdita Robinson and Lady Melbourne before meeting, in 1784, Maria Fitzherbert, a twice-widowed Catholic. Refusing his advances, she fled, but in 1785 they were secretly married, although the ceremony was invalid in the eyes of the law. George left her for Lady Jersey in 1794. The marriage was only ever known to a select few and the couple were reunited in 1800 before finally separating for good in 1811.

DISASTROUS MARRIAGE

Debt-ridden George struck a deal: if Parliament settled his debts, he would marry his cousin, Princess Caroline of Brunswick. He found her fat, vulgar and dirty. Drunk at and after the wedding in 1795, he then fell into the bedroom fireplace. Yet Caroline did bear a child, Princess Charlotte, although the couple soon separated. Popular with the public, unlike her husband, Queen Caroline led an erratic lifestyle, roaming Europe with a lover named Bartolomeo Pergami. She was shut out of Westminster Abbey on George's coronation day in 1821, and died shortly afterwards.

Broken by the death of Princess Charlotte in childbirth, the bloated, ageing George IV was dominated by his sinister doctor, Sir William Knighton. Dosed by laudanum taken in brandy, the king died surrounded by former mistresses and was succeeded by his brother William.

WILLIAM IV

William, sent to sea at 13, enjoyed a sailor's life and lived happily for 20 years with the famous actress Dorothea Jordan, who had ten of her 15 children with him. Nobody expected William, Duke of Clarence, to be king, but on Princess Charlotte's death in 1817, he yielded to family pressure, left Dorothea and joined his middle-aged brothers in scrambling to marry royally and sire an heir. 'Silly Billy's' wife, Adelaide of Saxe-Meiningen, had no children. The Duke of Kent fared better, producing the future Queen Victoria, but his death left William, at 64, the throne.

Overjoyed, King William went racing round London in his carriage, bowing this way and that, kissing strangers and offering them lifts. His sailors'

▲ A caricature from 1820 satirizing George IV's marital woes as 'A scene from Don Giovanni as perform'd at the Kings Theatre'.

▼ In the 'Triumph of Love and Folly' of 1812, Queen Caroline sits atop a sedan chair carrying a bloated Prince Regent.

language and habit of spitting upset courtiers, but William was no fool. He spent frugally compared to George IV, insisted on a simple coronation, and was more liberal in politics. His dislike of Victoria's mother led him to repeat rumours of her affair with Sir John Conroy, who ran her household – and determined him to live until Victoria should reach 18, the royal age of majority.

The VICTORIANS

Victoria's reign began in 1837, amid whispers of the suspected scandal between her widowed mother and Sir John Conroy. Some even claimed Conroy was Victoria's father.

THE HASTINGS AFFAIR

When Lady Flora Hastings (who knew Conroy well) showed symptoms suggesting pregnancy, she was forced to undergo a medical examination to prove her virginity. She was, in fact, ill and died of cancer soon after.

➤ Lady Flora Hastings, whose treatment following unfounded rumours of false pregnancy caused a court scandal.

FAMILY BACKGROUND

Albert of Saxe-Coburg, seemingly an ideal spouse for the young queen, had skeletons in his family cupboard. His parents, Ernest and Louise (both promiscuous), divorced in 1826, whereupon Ernest married his own niece (making Albert's cousin his stepmother). Tittle-tattle about Albert's parentage suggested his father was not Ernest at all, but one of Louise's lovers.

Victoria enjoyed married life, though she called pregnancy 'the shadow side'. She disapproved of too-frequent pregnancies, which were common, and regretted that 'we poor creatures [women] are born for Man's pleasure and amusement'. Even 'dear Papa' was 'not quite exempt'. Albert's death in 1861 sent the Queen into seclusion.

◄ Queen Victoria in her coronation robes.

JOHN BROWN AND THE MUNSHI

During Victoria's withdrawal, her relationship with her Scottish servant John Brown caused resentment. Foreign scandal-journals suggested a secret marriage. Royal doctor James Reid apparently kept a memo book referring to letters concerning Brown – but the book was burnt, so the nature of the royal letters is unknown. Court traditionalists were also annoyed by the rise of her favourite Indian servant, Abdul Karim, known as the Munshi. The queen saw this as snobbery, and rebutted all charges against the Munshi, including allegations that he was a spy and (worse) low-class. She indignantly retorted that she knew two archbishops whose fathers were, respectively, a butcher and a grocer.

▲ John Brown holds the bridle as the queen, in deepest black, goes riding.

NO HIGHLAND FLING

Brown was once on hand when a drunken coachman drove the queen into a ditch, giving her a black eye. US magazines claimed Brown was a spiritualist, helping the queen contact her dead husband. *Punch* published a satirical 'Brown's diary' detailing his intake of haggis. Court ladies noted his fondness for whisky, sometimes adding a nip to the queen's cup (she disliked tea, but would sip Brown's brew).

◀ Abdul Karim, Queen Victoria's favoured servant.

THE PRINCE OF WALES

'Bertie' (Edward, Prince of Wales) caused Victoria and Albert much anxiety. At 19, army comrades gifted him (in his tent) an actress, Nellie Clifden. Later, his wife Alexandra had to turn a blind eye to his various mistresses (including Alice Keppel and the stage star Lily Langtry), while the prince's 'Marlborough House set' was regarded as scandalously 'fast'. There were trips to Paris, visits to brothels, illegal card games, much smoking and eating (though relatively modest drinking). In 1870 the prince became involved in a messy court case. Sir Charles Mordaunt sought to divorce his wife for adultery; Lady Mordaunt cited the prince as one of her lovers, and he was called as a witness, admitting he had visited the lady in the afternoon, in her husband's absence. The court ruled Lady Mordaunt insane. The prince's reputation survived – though his mother's disapproval deepened.

THE BACCARAT SCANDAL

In 1890 Edward, in Yorkshire for the St Leger horse race, was playing cards at Tranby Croft. The game was Baccarat, and Colonel Sir William Gordon-Cumming was accused of cheating. Although other players tried to hush up the affair, news got out, and Sir William sued for slander. Edward was called to give evidence, amid much tut-tutting at his attending 'loose' parties, and (as a Field Marshal) failing to report a fellow officer's misconduct.

➤ Lily Langtry, the king's mistress.

SOCIETY SCANDALS

'Daisy', Lady Brooke (wife of a future Earl of Warwick), had an affair with Lord Charles Beresford, a naval officer and friend of the Prince of Wales. When his wife Mina became pregnant in 1889, Beresford tried to end the affair. But Daisy wrote demanding he leave Mina, who read the letter and went to her lawyer. Daisy appealed to the prince. He visited both the lawyer and Mina, demanding the letter, and threatening Lady Beresford with 'cutting' (social exclusion). Beresford called this 'most dishonourable', and the two men were never reconciled. In gratitude, Daisy transferred her favours to the prince. Never discreet, she was nicknamed 'the babbling Brooke'.

KING AT LAST

'Bertie' waited until 1901 to become King Edward VII. Then aged 59, more temperate and less robust in health, he devoted more time to diplomacy, becoming 'Edward the Peacemaker'. By the time he died, in 1910, his scrapes and scandals were largely forgotten, and forgiven.

▲ Daisy, Countess of Warwick (seated) with her family and pets at Warwick Castle.

➤ Edward VII on his deathbed. By this time he was a much-loved British figure.

The WINDSORS

George V never expected to be king. His somewhat dissolute older brother Albert ('Eddy') had become engaged to Princess Mary of Teck but died of pneumonia in 1892. George took his place, marrying Mary in 1893, and succeeding as king in 1910. Conservative, moral, and happiest when sailing, shooting, or poring over stamps, George V restored 'respectability' to the royal family. Mystery and sadness surrounded the family's youngest son, Prince John, who was born an invalid in 1905 and lived away from the public eye until his death in 1919.

▲ Prince John lived out of the public's gaze.

THE ABDICATION

Royal press coverage was deferentially discreet until the 1920s, when media interest was sparked by the life and loves of the Prince of Wales. Not at all conservative, he liked smart society, holidays and film stars. Aristocratic circles knew of his long-standing affair with Freda Dudley Ward, which ended abruptly when in 1931 he met Wallis Simpson, a twice-divorced American. Their relationship remained secret in Britain until 1936, when George V died and the boyish prince became king. It seemed that the new Edward VIII was set on marrying Mrs Simpson. Most of Parliament, the Church and the press urged him to think again. He refused. Choosing Mrs Simpson over kingship, he abdicated, and his shocked brother Albert, Duke of York, found himself King George VI.

▲ George V and Mary leaving St George's Chapel after their son Edward had been invested in the Order of the Garter, on 22 June 1911.

The four princes – the future kings Edward VIII and George VI, with their brothers Henry, Duke of Gloucester and George, Duke of Kent. This photograph was taken during the funeral procession of their father, George V.

A raffish-looking Prince of Wales on Derby Day, 1926.

A sporting photograph of the young man who would become King George VI – here, as a competitor in the Men's Doubles at Wimbledon.

EDWARD THE EXILE

Edward became HRH the Duke of Windsor, although his wife was not granted royal status. An imprudent visit to Germany in 1937 prompted charges of fascist sympathies, and the duke became an exile. He spent the war years as governor of the Bahamas, and until his death in 1972 lived mostly in France.

TODAY'S FAMILY

King George VI, Queen Elizabeth and their daughters, Elizabeth and Margaret, were thrust into the limelight. There were mild sensations, as when in 1950 royal nanny 'Crawfie' (Marion Crawford) published a book about her charges, but when the king died in 1952, the royal family's reputation had been restored by wartime service. The new Queen Elizabeth II presented a fresh image, of a young mother with a growing family. Princess Margaret was less fortunate; her wish to marry Peter Townsend, a wartime fighter ace, was thwarted because he was divorced and therefore unsuitable in establishment eyes. Her eventual marriage, to Anthony Armstrong-Jones, ended in divorce, as did the marriages of three of the queen's children. The separation of Prince Charles and Princess Diana in 1996 caught the full glare of media attention, amid revelations of leaked taped messages, secret phone calls, and lovers.

▲ Princess Elizabeth with Lieutenant Philip Mountbatten on their engagement, July 1947.

◀ Lady Elizabeth Bowes-Lyon married the Duke of York in 1923, and became queen in 1936, when her husband became King George VI.

▼ At a London theatre in the late 1940s (from left to right): young Princess Margaret, King George VI, Queen Elizabeth, Group Captain Peter Townsend and Princess Elizabeth.

DEATH IN PARIS

Diana, Princess of Wales died in 1997 after a Paris car crash, a tragedy fuelling rumours and conspiracy theories. The official cause of the crash was high speed and an alcohol-affected chauffeur, and a later police inquiry (Operation Paget) found no evidence to contradict this.

NEW GENERATION

In the present century, royal fortunes have never been sunnier, as a new generation takes the stage, with the public and media generally approving and congratulatory. In 2015, the queen surpassed Victoria as Britain's longest-reigning monarch. Scandals and secrets of the past have often lain undiscovered, sometimes for centuries. However, today's digital-information age, and intense press interest, may perhaps suggest that such secrecy can no longer exist.

▲ Prince Charles and Princess Diana of Wales.

▼ Prince George makes his first public appearance in July 2013.

PLACES TO VISIT

There is space to mention only a few of the many places in the United Kingdom with links to royal history, including royal palaces and fortresses, national museums and historic houses:

Battle Abbey and 1066 Battlefield
High St, Battle, Hastings and Battle, East Sussex
TN33 0AD
www.english-heritage.org.uk/visit/places/1066-battle-of-hastings-abbey-and-battlefield/

Buckingham Palace
London SW1A 1AA
www.royal.gov.uk/theroyalresidences/buckinghampalace/buckinghampalace.aspx

Caernarfon Castle
Pen Deitsh, Caernarfon, Gwynedd LL55 2AY
www.caernarfon-castle.co.uk

Canterbury Cathedral
Cathedral House, 11 The Precincts, Canterbury, Kent
CT1 2EH
www.canterbury-cathedral.org

Dover Castle
Castle Hill, Dover, Kent CT16 1HU
www.english-heritage.org.uk/visit/places/dover-castle

Edinburgh Castle
Castlehill, Edinburgh EH1 2NG
www.edinburghcastle.gov.uk

Hampton Court Palace
East Molesey, Surrey KT8 9AU
www.hrp.org.uk/hampton-court-palace

Hardwick Hall
Doe Lea, Chesterfield, Derbyshire S44 5QJ
www.nationaltrust.org.uk/hardwick-hall

Hever Castle
Hever Rd, Hever, Edenbridge, Kent TN8 7NG
www.hevercastle.co.uk

Kenilworth Castle
Castle Green, Kenilworth, Warwickshire CV8 1NE
www.english-heritage.org.uk/visit/places/kenilworth-castle

Kensington Palace
Kensington Gardens, London W8 4PX
www.hrp.org.uk/kensington-palace

Runnymede
Windsor Rd, Old Windsor, Windsor, Surrey SL4 2JL
www.nationaltrust.org.uk/runnymede

Stirling Castle
Stirling Castle, Castle Esplanade, Stirling FK8 1EJ
www.stirlingcastle.gov.uk

Tower of London
London EC3N 4AB
www.hrp.org.uk/tower-of-london

Warwick Castle, Warwickshire
Warwick CV34 4QU
www.warwick-castle.com

Westminster Abbey
20 Dean's Yard, London SW1P 3PA
www.westminster-abbey.org

Windsor Castle
Windsor, Windsor and Maidenhead SL4 1NJ
www.royalcollection.org.uk/visit/windsorcastle